TRAVELING THE
Blue Road
POEMS OF THE SEA

COLLECTED BY

Lee Bennett Hopkins

ILLUSTRATED BY

Bob Hansman & Jovan Hansman

SEAGRASS PRESS/LAKE FOREST, CA

To Judith Mandell and Stephanie Salkin
for our traveled roads.
—LBH

Brimming with creative inspiration, how-to projects, and useful information to enrich your everyday life, Quarto Knows is a favorite destination for those pursuing their interests and passions. Visit our site and dig deeper with our books into your area of interest: Quarto Creates, Quarto Cooks, Quarto Homes, Quarto Lives, Quarto Drives, Quarto Explores, Quarto Gifts, or Quarto Kids.

© 2017 Quarto Publishing Group USA Inc.
Compilation © 2017 Lee Bennett Hopkins
Credits for each poem and for images used within the illustrations are found on page 31.

First Published in 2017 by Seagrass Press, an imprint of The Quarto Group.
6 Orchard Road, Suite 100, Lake Forest, CA 92630, USA.
T (949) 380-7510 F (949) 380-7575 **www.QuartoKnows.com**

Library of Congress Cataloging in Publication Data has been applied for.

Seagrass Press titles are also available at discount for retail, wholesale, promotional, and bulk purchase. For details, contact the Special Sales Manager by email at specialsales@quarto.com or by mail at The Quarto Group, Attn: Special Sales Manager, 401 Second Avenue North, Suite 310, Minneapolis, MN 55401 USA.

ISBN: 978-1-63322-276-2

Designed by Kathleen Westray

Printed in China
10 9 8 7 6 5 4 3 2 1

CONTENTS

INTRODUCTION

Standing on a balcony during a recent Caribbean cruise, I gazed across endless miles of water. The sea—awesome, breathtaking, frightening, filled with wonder—has always beckoned dreamers from shore to shore who have, as Rebecca Kai Dotlich phrases it in her poem "Sea," "traveled away from, / traveled toward . . ." The sea has also carried less willing travelers across its wide expanses, both those compelled by hard circumstances to brave its blue distances and those captured into bondage to make bleak, terrifying crossings.

Traveling the Blue Road: Poems of the Sea features fourteen poems specially commissioned and written for this collection. The work traces various voyages throughout history, depicting how sea adventures can be alluring, luring—or dreadfully deadly. Each poet delved into a specific topic to create diverse verse as sweeping as the sea itself. Meticulously crafted poems stir us, shake us, cause us to think, wander, ponder, imagining what might have been, bringing to life imagery only poets can convey via the power of words—sailors in Paul B. Janeczko's poem "Voyage" suffering "flea bites as common as rain"; a young girl captured as a slave in Marilyn Nelson's poem "Kidnapped by Aliens" "curled around terror, facing the blue unknown"; passengers in Georgia Heard's poem "The Hunger Ship: 1847" "dazed, dirty, stench in every pore."

Notes at the end of the collection place the voyage it depicts in context, exploring tumultuous events in history, shedding light on the trials and tribulations humans have dealt with, and will continue to deal with, via the sweeping, whispering, clinging sea.

Lee Bennett Hopkins
CAPE CORAL, FLORIDA

SEA
Rebecca Kai Dotlich

Wistful with wind and North Star,
the sea sailed steamships,
drifted dinghies,
battered fishing boats,
barges, homemade rafts
beneath a breath
of gray stars.

Steering the stoic, the brave,
the weary that clutched small hands
and cold compasses in cramped fists,
oceans stamped passages
with sunburn and storms
as blackswept swells
    rolled *forward, back,*
       forward, back.

The sea pulled sailors
over salty swells,
opened its mouth wide,
swallowed splinters of rail, hull,
shipwrecks, bones.
Dreamers lurched along;
swaying vessels of seekers
haunted by grit of night,
soothed by light of day;
sweeping them choppily
from shore to shore;
traveled a*way from,*
   traveled toward . . .

"My soul is full of longing
for the secret of the sea."
—*Henry Wadsworth Longfellow*

VOYAGE

Paul B. Janeczko

From Spain
the ships rode waves
that whispered against
    wooden hulls.
Barefooted men
worked with fear
a constant companion
that a sea monster might
    splinter a ship
scattering supplies and sailors,
that food would run out
before the ships harbored
that mice and rats would bite
men sleeping on deck.

For weeks sailors worked,
happy at first
with visions of wealth untold
Indies would give them.

Tedium of such a voyage grew
with each passing watch.
Five weeks, then six,
longer by far
than usual for cargo
    ships.
And still they did
    their work
always with a glance
at the horizon
for signs of land.
Scrubbing decks,
mending railings.

And always sails
loosening
tightening
raising
lowering
under sun
pewter skies
or stormy skies
as black as the deepest
corner of the hold.
The sails.
Always the sails.

Eating at night
to avoid seeing
maggots wriggling
through beans
or salted meat.

Fear growing
like a thunderhead.
After eight weeks
lice in their hair
flea bites as common as rain.
Sailors speak of turning back,
calmed by the captain's words
of riches on the horizon.

Whispers of mutiny
as their home becomes
a cramped and
    filthy prison.

At last
at eight weeks
signs appear:
land birds circle
    the ship
calling at night.
Branches and
    boughs drift by.

All eyes looking west
until a sailor on
    the *Pinta*
sings out, *"¡Tierra!
    ¡Tierra!"*
A cannon thunders
to alert other ships.

Joy fills the sailors.
Some weep.
Some dance.
Some offer a prayer
    of thanks
For deliverance
To a new world.

*"You can never cross the ocean
until you have courage to
lose sight of the shore."*
—*Christopher Columbus*

CARGO

J. Patrick Lewis

Dutch ships were paid to violate the sea
through passages bound for oblivion.
Their openless cargo, black humanity,

endured the brutal crimes of slavery,
starvation, cat-o'-nine tails, and the gun.

Dutch ships were paid to violate the sea.

The sea in turn pretended not to be
concerned, as waves transported run by run
more hopeless cargo: black humanity.

"The sea must know
more than any of us."
—*Carl Sandburg*

WITH FEARLESS FAITH
AND EVERYTHING TO LOSE

Allan Wolf

One hundred and two hopeful souls all climb aboard,
with thirty or so salty dogs to crew them on.
One hundred and two faces turn upward to the Lord.
One hundred and two prayers blow windward and they're gone.
One hundred and two faithful huddle in the hold,
amidst the massive sea, their ship a fragile fleck.
The mainmast cracks. The heathen winds harass and scold.
The brutal cold Atlantic swamps the sagging deck.
But through the mist and foam they somehow reach the land.
And cradled safe (for now) at last in Cape Cod Bay,
their pilgrim journey ends the same as it began:
with one hundred and two facing heavenward to pray.
They risked it all to worship as they choose,
with fearless faith and everything to lose.

KIDNAPPED BY ALIENS

Marilyn Nelson

I was hiding in the bush when Papa got killed.
His machete was no match for the aliens.
Their weapons thundered as villagers screamed
for their gods to hear them—be merciful.
But the gods of the aliens were more powerful.
Wherever they came from, their gods must have come with them.

At sunset, silence fell on our village.
Thirst, hunger forced me to creep out
into a nightmare of devastation.
All I saw moving were chickens and skinny dogs
nosing around for scraps. I put a cloth
on Papa's face. I closed my eyes to pray.

That's when the aliens grabbed me. They marched us
up hill and down, yelling in their language,
pushing, lashing us, taking women
into the woods, leaving behind the old.
We reached a body of water as vast as the sky.
They locked us for days in a huge house made of stones.

When they brought us out, sunlight blinded me.
I followed others up a slanting ramp
into the craft that had brought the aliens
from wherever they came from to our peaceful world.
That was my last glimpse of the world. In here
darkness, sickness, clanking chains, whispering.

Where are they taking us? Will we be food?
Did they come across the water? Did they come from a star?
In the place they come from, is evil good?
Will I ever see my mother again?
My little sister? My brothers? My best friend?
I lie curled around terror, facing the blue unknown.

"Pity us, pity the ocean, here we go."
—Ann Carson

MARGARET
(Aboard the *Margaret*)
Denver Butson

I never thought the sea was mine to see
those soot-choked streets those
    dung-stench streets
at my machine before the sun and
    not back out
until after whatever sun there was
    or wasn't
but then I stole a heel of bread from
    the bakery cart
and rolled it in my apron and walked
and was cuffed before I even got a
    single block
and the bread wasn't even for me
    but for my ma
at home with another one coming
    in her belly
another one to claw for crumbs
another one to rap her knuckles
    against its head
another one to hold to her grimy
    breast
and weep and heave and weep and
    heave
another one to promise
someday dearie someday we will live
*   near the sea*
just like she promised me
though I tried but could not believe
    her even then
because I never thought the sea was
    mine to see

"The sea . . . Greys
everything, crushes everything,
cleans everything, takes
everything from me."
—*Corinne Bailey Rae*

I never thought the sea was mine
　　to see
and yet here I am
out here on this creaking deck
on a ship I pretend with all my
　　might was named for me
and at first I could barely see the
　　sea as the sea
waves of fabric to smooth
as if I could flatten wrinkled water
white stitches rising up
until I realized they were birds
a needle there and another there
　　glinting
that weren't needles at all
but flashes of sun off the sea
here I am yanked up from the
　　down below

miles it seems from the hands that grab
miles from the mouths that yearn
　　and moan

here I am able to sit for a while with my
　　face in the sun
to scare the scurvy out of ye to kill them
　　critters
the kind one who calls himself Thomas
　　tells me
but I like to think that they bring me up
for more than this
that these moments of waves and birds
　　and sun
are so I have something to believe
other than that dark is dark is dark
something to believe other than that
the sea was never mine to see

THE HUNGER SHIP: 1847

Georgia Heard

A few hundred passengers stood on deck,
sending sorrowful kisses, solemn prayers
over ship's wake, into misty air.

Ninety days they slept
four to a bunk in a dark hull.
Dazed, dirty, stench in every pore.

Hunger took small bites out of hope.

Their coffin ship ploughed the ocean,
under freezing stars,
like they once ploughed barren fields.

What lay between Ireland and their dreams
was a burial ground lined with crosses,
a deep, unfathomable faith
as wailing wind piped a melancholy seisún.

seisún (seh-shoon): a gathering of musicians to play traditional Irish music

TITAN

Lee Bennett Hopkins

I was *Titanic*
   the largest
   most luxurious ship
   the world had ever known.

I was the liner serving
   soda scones with Oxford
   marmalade
   filet mignon
   lamb with mint sauce
   tapioca and plum pudding
   to a very special class of
   passengers.

Men, women, children,
   dogs, cats,
   birds, rats
   millionaires
   dowagers
   dignitaries
   celebrities
   servants
   and refugees
   roamed my vastness.

I was the one who gave—
   still gives—
   will forevermore
   gift historians with so much
   poetic prose to pen . . .

sailing ship of fantasy dreams . . .

through a breathtaking glass dome
sunlight streams . . .

people dressed in finest garb waltz
down a staircase from way up
high . . .

calm, motionless seas under
a crystal-clear, moonless sky . . .

Now—
   more than a century ago—
   now—
   I no longer was
   but am
   as I continue to
   fascinate, captivate,
   thrill, titillate—
   will eternally be
   the titan of the sea.

You will forever—
remember
me.

"The sea, the sea, the sea. It rolled
and rolled and called to me.
Come in, it said, *come in.*"
—Sharon Creech

BLUE THE COLOR OF HOPE: On the Ship *St. Louis*

Jane Yolen

Blue road the color of hope,
Waves like *tzitzit* on a prayer shawl,
Sea lanes our only map.

Sea lanes our only map,
We speak the *Sh'ma* into the air.
It whispers back promises.

It whispers back promises
Sweet as the honey
On the *alef bet* slate.

On the *alef bet* slate
We licked the honey off,
Our first hunger for knowledge.

Our first hunger for knowledge
Did not lead us to understand
The depth of hate.

The depth of hate
Pushed us onto this boat
Where blue is the color of hope.

tzitzit: fringes or tassels
Sh'ma: Jewish prayer service
alef bet: a Hebrew alphabet

RETURN TO THE REICH: On the Ship *St. Louis*

Jane Yolen

Even Cuba did not want us,
Denying immigrant papers,
Sending us back on the blue road.

Sending us back on the blue road,
This time to Florida where lights
Of Miami sent Morse signals.

Miami sent Morse signals
Denying us entrance.
Waving us back towards Germany.

Waving us back towards Germany,
Where all the windows
And lights of Kristallnacht were broken.

The lights of Kristallnacht were broken
Shattered like our lives,
Strong warnings of what was to come.

Strong warnings of what was to come
Had sent us into exile,
    our homes behind us,
And the horror of the ovens ahead.

The horror of the ovens ahead
Yet to be revealed,
We chanced the blue road again.

We chanced the blue road again,
Waves like bony fingers of ghosts.
Drowning would have been a softer death.

Drowning would have been a softer death.
But even then prayers did not suffice,
For we were sent back home.

We were sent back home
To a place where murderers waited.
Even Cuba did not want us.

CARRIED ON SWAYING WAVES OF HOPE

Margarita Engle

Adiós, Mariel, crowded port
where boats swoop like seabirds,
each vessel filled up with people
who dream of seeing *primos, tíos y amigos*
on the far shore
in La Florida,
where we will soon
celebrate a fiesta
with plenty to eat
and freedom to speak
of our past, present, future

as families
reunited . . .

but still divided.

Adiós, Abuelita, adiós.
Will I ever see my grandma
again?

adiós: good-bye
primos, tíos y amigos: cousins, uncles, aunts, and friends

MEDITERRANEAN BLUE
Naomi Shihab Nye

If you are the child of a refugee, you do not
sleep easily when they are crossing the sea
on small rafts and you know they can't swim.
My father couldn't swim either. He swam through
sorrow, though, and made it to the other side
on a ship, pitching his old clothes overboard
at landing, then tried to be happy, make a new life.
But something inside him was always paddling home,
clinging to anything that floated—a story, a food or face.
They are the bravest people on earth right now,
don't dare look down on them. Each mind a universe
swirling as many details as yours, as much love for
a humble place. Now the shirt is torn,
the sea too wide for comfort, and nowhere
to receive a letter for a very long time.

And if we can reach out a hand, we better.

"We are tied
to the ocean . . ."
—*John F. Kennedy*

MEN OF WAVES AND SEA

G. Neri

Father hates going to land.

They treat us like beggars,
Call us sea gypsies, outcasts,
The Spat Out.

Father is too proud.
He refuses to live
In stilted hut shanty towns
Set up for people who have lost
The life of the sea.
He gets land sick just thinking
    about it
Because the ground does not roll
    and sway;
It does not breathe
Like the ocean.
Land people are locked into

For us, the sea is an open road
We are meant to roam, to be free
Like the fish and octopus we hunt.
It is the old way, the way of our
    people,
Only the old way is dying:
Fish from pollution,
Us from the warring Mindanao.
When food is scarce,
I dive for coins from passing tourists.
But our worst enemy is pirates.

One day,
After hours spear fishing underwater,
Father hears a motorboat
    approaching.
Pirates!

Our boat is too slow to outrun them.
They will kill us for our haul,
For our monthly stipend.
There is only one escape from pirates:

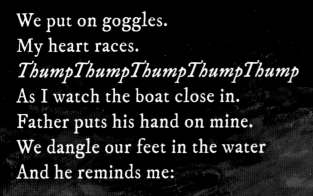

We put on goggles.
My heart races.
ThumpThumpThumpThumpThump
As I watch the boat close in.
Father puts his hand on mine.
We dangle our feet in the water
And he reminds me:

We are the Sama Dilaut.
We are born, live, and die by the sea.
She is our provider and our protector.

We slow our breath, close our eyes.
I listen to the sound of waves
Lapping against the side of the boat
Until we are one with the sea.

Down we go,
Our lungs half full so we sink to
 the bottom
Out of danger.
Under the waves, all is quiet.
High above I see the motorboat pull up
And our *kabang* rocks as they board.

Father taught me to hold my breath
For five minutes.
It is what we do when we walk the
 ocean floor
Collecting sea urchins and shells
 for tourists.

Now, we are waiting for danger
 to pass.
Waiting for the end of conflict.
Waiting for the fish to return.
The sea people are almost gone
But we, the last few
Men of waves and sea,
Remain.

For now
We wait
And hope Mother Sea
Will give us one more
Day.

Sama Dilaut: the sea-going Sama people
kabang: a long, hollow boat

AFT

"The sea always in my ear."
—Keri Hulme

SEAS SEAS
Lee Bennett Hopkins

Seas seas seas seas seas seas seas seas

Seas seas sweeping seas whispering seas

seas seas violating seas massive seas unknown seas

seas seas smooth seas unfathomable seas titan seas

seas seas blue seas warning seas swooping seas

seas seas clinging seas breathing seas

seas seas seas seas seas seas seas seas

NOTES

The Fifteenth Century

Columbus's Voyage, 1492

Commanding three ships, the *Pinta*, the *Niña*, and the *Santa Maria*, Christopher Columbus departed from Palos, Spain, on August 3, 1492. After a long, arduous journey, land was spotted on October 12, 1492, by Juan Rodríguez Bermejo, also known as Rodrigo de Triana, a lookout aboard the *Pinta*.

The arrival of Columbus and his crews in the Caribbean would have a devastating effect on the native cultures and peoples they encountered, including the introduction of diseases, forced conversions, and other forms of exploitation.

The Seventeenth Century

The Dutch Slave Trade, 1619

On August 20, 1619, about twenty African captives arrived in Jamestown, Virginia, becoming the first Africans to set foot in North America and marking the beginning of African slave trade.

The *Mayflower*, 1620

On September 6, 1620, the *Mayflower* sailed from Southampton, England, transporting the first English Separatists, known as Pilgrims, seeking religious freedom in America. They reached what is now Provincetown, Massachusetts, on November 9, 1620. Before coming ashore, forty-one men signed the Mayflower Compact, a 200-word document that established a temporary government, pledging the signers to be bound by its laws.

The Eighteenth Century

The Middle Passage

The sea voyage of enslaved Africans to the Americas as part of the Transatlantic slave trade was called the Middle Passage. These voyages represent the largest movement of people in history. Many of those taken into bondage had never been on a ship before or even seen the sea. Those abducted were viewed as cargo, or goods, by their captors.

The Nineteenth Century

The *Margaret*, 1837

Between 1788 and 1868, about 162,000 convicts were transported by the British government to penal colonies in Australia, areas where prisoners were exiled, often located on unsettled islands from which escape was nearly impossible. The transport ship *Margaret* left Cork, Ireland, on January 24, 1837, and arrived in Port Jackson, in Sydney, Australia, on May 30. Most of the 200 passengers were female prisoners

Irish Potato Famine, 1845–1852

The Irish Potato Famine, caused by a repeated failure of potato crops due to a blight, lasted from 1845 to 1852 and stands among the world's greatest humanitarian disasters. Over a million Irish people died, and another million fled to America, often in crowded ships with poor sanitation.

The Twentieth Century

The *Titanic*, 1912

The *Titanic*, a British passenger liner, sank in the North Atlantic Ocean on April 15, 1912. Of the 2,224 passengers and crew aboard, more than 1,500 died, making the voyage one of the deadliest peacetime maritime disasters in modern history.

The Voyage of MS *St. Louis*, 1939

On May 13, 1939, MS *St. Louis*, a German ocean liner, sailed from Hamburg, Germany, to Havana, Cuba, with more than 900 Jewish refugees seeking asylum from Nazi persecution. Upon reaching Havana on May 27, they were denied entry and forced to return to Europe.

In the years following their return to Europe, more than 250 of the *St. Louis* refugees died in Nazi concentration camps. In the poem earlier, Kristallnacht, or "The Night of Broken Glass," refers to a pogrom in November 1938, when thirty thousand Jews were arrested and sent to the camps. Between 1939 and 1945, Adolf Hitler and the Nazis implemented what they called a "Final Solution" to the "Jewish Problem," murdering some six million Jews in a period known as the Holocaust.

The Mariel Boat Lift, 1980

On April 20, 1980, Fidel Castro announced that all Cubans wishing to emigrate to the United States were free to board boats at the port of Mariel, resulting in a mass emigration of Cubans to America. Over the next six months, more than 125,000 Cubans reached Florida.

The Twenty-first Century

Mediterranean Refugee Crisis, 2014

In 2014, more than 200,000 refugees were rescued trying to cross the Mediterranean Sea from Africa and the Middle East to Europe. It is estimated that between April 13 and 21, 2015, as many as 1,300 refugees perished when small overcrowded boats sank during these trips.

The Sama-Bajau, Present Day

For generations, the Sama-Bajau people of Southeast Asia have spent their entire lives on the ocean, depending on the sea for their subsistence and living on *vintas*, small houseboats that travel in flotillas. Long considered outcasts by predominant ethnic groups, they remain nomads of the sea, rarely setting foot, or being welcomed, on land. In recent years, governments in the Philippines have made efforts to assist impoverished Sama-Bajau people and teach them new livelihood skills.

ABOUT THE POETS

Denver Butson has written several books of poetry for adults. His poems appear in numerous journals and anthologies. He lives in New York.

Rebecca Kai Dotlich is the author of numerous poetry and picture books, including *One Day, the End*, a Boston Globe–Horn Book Honor Book. Her work is widely anthologized. She lives in Indiana.

Margarita Engle is the author of many books of poetry, including *The Surrender Tree*, a Newbery Honor Book, and *Enchanted Air*, recipient of the 2016 Lee Bennett Hopkins Poetry Award. Much of her work draws on her Cuban-American heritage. In May 2017, she was named the Young People's Poet Laureate by the Poetry Foundation. She lives in California.

Georgia Heard, a founding member of Columbia University Teachers College Reading and Writing Project, has traveled worldwide as a consultant, author, and keynote speaker. She has compiled anthologies for all ages and has written professional books for teachers. She lives in Florida.

Lee Bennett Hopkins has compiled more than one hundred anthologies and been recognized by Guinness World Records as the most prolific anthologist of poetry for children. In 2017, he was inducted into the Florida Artists Hall of Fame. He has received many awards, including the Christopher Award, the Regina Medal, and the National Council of Teachers of English Award for Excellence in Poetry for Children. He lives in Florida.

Paul B. Janeczko taught high school students for twenty-two years before leaving the profession to focus on poetry. An eminent anthologist of children's and young adult collections, he lives in Maine.

J. Patrick Lewis is the author of scores of poetry volumes and the compiler of numerous poetry anthologies. From 2011 to 2013, he served as the third US Children's Poet Laureate. He is recipient of the National Council of Teachers of English Award for Excellence in Poetry for Children. He lives in Ohio.

Marilyn Nelson, former Poet Laureate of Connecticut and a winner of the Frost Medal, received the 2017 National Council of Teachers of English Award for Excellence in Poetry for Children. She is the author of many books of poetry, including *Carver*, a Newbery Honor Book, and *My Seneca Village*, a Lee Bennett Hopkins Poetry Award Honor Book. She lives in Connecticut.

G. Neri received a Coretta Scott King Author Honor for his verse novel *Yummy* and is a recipient of the International Reading Association Lee Bennett Hopkins Promising Poet Award for his free-verse novella, *Chess Rumble*. He lives in Florida.

Naomi Shihab Nye is a multi-award-winning poet who writes for all ages. Her collection *19 Varieties of Gazelle: Poems of the Middle East* was a finalist for the National Book Award. She lives in Texas.

Allan Wolf is an educator, writer, and musician. His highly acclaimed verse novel *New Found Land: Lewis and Clark's Voyage of Discovery* was a Lion and Unicorn Award for Excellence in North American Poetry Honor winner. He lives in North Carolina.

Jane Yolen, an icon in the field of children's literature, writes for all ages. Among her many awards are the Regina Medal and the Christopher Award. Her classic picture book *Owl Moon* received a Caldecott Medal. She lives in Massachusetts.

ACKNOWLEDGMENTS

Thanks are due to the following for use of works in this collection:

Curtis Brown, Ltd. for "Sea" by Rebecca Kai Dotlich, copyright © 2017 by Rebecca Kai Dotlich;
"The Hunger Ship : 1847" by Georgia Heard, copyright © 2017 by Georgia Heard;
"Titan" and "Sea Seas" by Lee Bennett Hopkins, copyright © 2017 by Lee Bennett Hopkins;
"Cargo" by J. Patrick Lewis, copyright © 2017 by J. Patrick Lewis;
"Blue is the Color of Hope: On the Ship *St. Louis*" and "Return to the Reich:
On the Ship *St. Louis*", copyright © 2017 by Jane Yolen.

All other works are used by permission of the respective poets, who control all rights;
all copyright © 2017: Denver Butson for " Margaret: Aboard the *Margaret*";
Margarita Engle for "Carried on Swaying Waves of Hope";
Paul B. Janeczko for "Voyage";
Marilyn Nelson for "Kidnapped by Aliens";
G. Neri for "Men of Waves and Sea";
Naomi Shihab Nye for "Mediterranean Blue";
Allan Wolf for "With Fearless Faith and Everything to Lose".

Special thanks to Josalyn Moran for this incredible voyage
and to Regina Griffin for unexpected waves of nostalgia.
—L.B.H.

PHOTO CREDITS

Images within the illustrations are reprinted with gratitude to the following institutions:

pp. 6-7: Columbus's landing from the Library of Congress/3g04188v;
Christopher Columbus from the Library of Congress/4a31476v.jpg;
p. 8: Jamestown from Getty Images/56248520;
p. 9: The *Mayflower* from Shutterstock/107991335;
p. 11: Deck of a slave ship c. 1860 from the Library of Congress/3a42003r;
captives from Shutterstock/218073364; ship from Shutterstock/237239767;
pp. 12-13: Convict ship c. 1787, WikiCommons; poorhouse from Getty Images/534233360;
pp. 14-15: All images from Emigrants Leave Ireland by Henry Doyle, c. 1868,
from WikiCommons;
pp. 16-17: The *Titanic* from Shutterstock/237232216; orphans of the *Titanic*
from the Library of Congress/11222v;
pp. 18-19: Refugees fleeing Nazi Germany from Getty Images/3368836;
pp. 20-21: Ship and three figures from Dr. Antonio Rafael de la Cova;
inset of marine and child by Fernando Yovera /AP through NBC News;
pp. 22-23: Refugees from Shutterstock/367744034; background of Emma Lazarus poem
on Statue of Liberty from the National Park Service;
pp. 24-25: Sama-Bajau child from Flickr/4766088274_0b95d2d0d1_o

ABOUT THIS BOOK

The artwork

Bob Hansman & Jovan Hansman bounced ideas back and forth, and also bounced drawings back and forth. Pastels are the main medium, but charcoal, charcoal pencil, colored pencil, Conte crayon, ink markers, and cut paper are also present. The images evolved over the course of the book, beginning with an entirely "archival" image, gradually blending archival images with drawn images, and ending with entirely drawn images. Although each detail is factually "correct," the ways in which the details combine become increasingly poetic and abstract, dream-like, going for a parallel or visual equivalent of the poems and emotions rather than literal illustration. After the original artwork was scanned as high-resolution files for the printing process, some additional Photoshop effects were applied.

The type

The various type fonts used throughout the book are based on authentic-looking text families from the past:

American Scribe: The Declaration of Independence was authored by Thomas Jefferson, but the copies' classic handwriting is not his. That belonged to Timothy Matlack (1736–1826), a Philadelphia brewer and master penman, who also penned copies of documents for General George Washington. In 1776, when the Continental Congress ordered the Declaration to be "fairly engrossed on parchment," the task fell to Matlack, whose script was compact but neat and legible—perfect for the first and most famous of American documents. This type font is an authentic simulation of that penmanship.

Attic Antique: simulates the rough, broken type from a 100-year-old textbook . . . a purposely uneven, imperfect, and weathered look.

Broadsheet: has the authentic look of the text-type printed in old newspapers and is based on antique American publications from 1728 to 1776. The term broadsheet derives from the large newspaper format of popular prints, usually of a single sheet, sold on the streets. The first broadsheet newspaper was published in 1618.

American Scribe, Attic Antique, and Broadsheet were designed by Brian Wilson of Three Islands Press, known for its library of authentic-looking handwritten fonts—most of them modeled after historical penmanship—and antique text-type simulations.

IM Fell DW Pica: The Fell types take their name from John Fell, a Bishop of Oxford in the seventeenth-century, who created a unique collection of printing type. Fell also decided to develop types and Peter De Walpergen became his personal type-founder, entrusted with the original cuts. The technical imperfection is part of the character of Fell types and consist of typographic "errors" such as variable serifs, inconsistent heights and slant angles, and different weights.

The Fell Types are digitally reproduced by Igino Marini.